Passive Digital Income

MAX CHAHUA

DEDICATION

To my beloved family.

CONTENTS

ACKNOWLEDGMENTS

To all the people who positively influenced my life

1 INTRODUCTION

We are in the twenty-first century. Passive income has always existed over the years, but the novelty of this twenty-first century is that you can earn completely digital passive income through the internet.

Imagine three hundred years ago or five hundred years ago that people did not have this opportunity, we who live in the twenty-first century if we have this opportunity.

Today in the XXI century, we can travel and fly through the air something that the kings of three hundred years ago could not, we can communicate over the internet and we can communicate by cell phone.

Today we are in the information age.

The internet was created in 1993, the internet is a product of the information age it is said that the industrial age ended with the fall of the Berlin wall and that the information age emerged from there.

In the twenty-first century there are many people who do not take advantage of this opportunity, this book is precisely for that, to see the opportunities we have to generate passive income in the information age.

Passive income from real estate is a product of the agrarian age.

Passive income from dividends is a product of the industrial era (dividends were born when companies were born, and they begin to pay dividends to their shareholders)

With the arrival of the information age, these types of income were modernized.

For example: dividends today are simply deposited into your account automatically and you receive an email, indicating that the deposit was made in your bank account, it is no longer necessary to go to collect or claim your check as it was done before in the industrial age, and the process is completely automatic.

And as for real estate, the rental of them is being almost completely automated, and you can also use companies like Airbnb to rent your real estate, which greatly automates the process of renting and paying rent.

Today many passive incomes have been partially or totally digitized, we also have what I call pure passive digital income, which is exactly what this book is about.

That is to say, income, exclusively from the information age, these are income that was born solely and exclusively in the information age.

This book will cover 10 of this digital passive income that we have to take advantage of.

This new era, that is, the information age began in the year that the internet began, which is 1993, we are currently in the 21st century

What did I mean by that?

That the world we live in, that in the age we live in is not even 50 years old!

In other words, this new era, as with the birth of each new era, is an era of great business opportunities to make a lot of money because the world is less than 50 years old!

Imagine how the industrial age started. All the new opportunities and money that could be made?

It's the same now! We have many opportunities and a lot of money can be made in this new information age!

You can generate a lot of money for a reason and that is that there are many opportunities to exploit, there are many things that still need to be created and built.

If you take advantage of them, well you can take advantage of the advantages that the information age offers, however, if you stick to the old ideas of the industrial age, you can be left behind.

As I write this, we are in the midst of the coronavirus pandemic.

And an example of this, of what I mention, are the Commercial Properties for rent.

While in the industrial era, commercial premises were a symbol of prestige and presence of a company.

Today in many cases they are a great liability for companies, since they increase their operating costs.

And it puts them at a disadvantage compared to those who sell through the internet (ecommerce) without having a physical location, which can offer lower prices and discounts because they do not have these expenses.

If you bought this book it is precisely because you see that, you are seeing something that some refuse to see, you know that there are opportunities that the information age offers.

In this book I will mention different sources of passive income, available to all of us.

This income can be obtained from the comfort of your home or office, and you can receive income from anywhere in the world. You could be cooking, eating or sleeping and at the same time be receiving passive income!

For example: When I sell books through Amazon, I do it automatically, I just check my account, and voila!

I have several books sold.

In some cases, I have sold many books while I was sleeping, and I am not kidding.

Let me tell you a real anecdote that happened to me recently with the sale of books through Amazon:

A weekend ago I fell asleep in the afternoon, when I woke up, I opened my Amazon KDP book library (where I have all the books that I have written), and to my surprise I had had several purchases of my book, while I was sleeping!!

Can you believe that? I was literally sleeping and still generating income!

Do you think that in an era prior to the current one (the industrial age, the agrarian age) doing this was possible?

Well, I doubt it a lot, maybe you could automate businesses and companies with the use people workforce, in previous times, but not in the way that can be done now, with fully digitized distribution and sales systems.

I was fascinated and realized that this is one that we can take advantage of.

Remember that the world is less than 50 years old.

We are in new times.

As I write this book, today, I can see people taking advantage of the internet and the tools that social media offers to increase their income.

Many of these people are young, some do not even reach the age of 25, and they take advantage of the opportunities offered by the internet and social networks.

But I also see the opposite side, people who cling to the past, who hope that everything will go back to the way it was before, when everything has already changed.

Economists call it "the new normality."

Robert Kiyosaki, author of Rich Dad Poor Dad, in his books mentions that there are two types of people:

-Those who cling to old ideas (secure employment, paid retirement from the company) will suffer in the future, because these ideas were industrial-age ideas that can no longer be applied due to competitiveness and globalization.

And that there will be more and more staff reductions, salary reductions, job losses due to the replacement of robots, outsourcing of work by workers who earn less in emerging countries among others.

-Those that make thousands of dollars - There is another group that will be making millions through their passive and digital income, taking advantage of the opportunities offered by the digital age.

The passive digital income that I will mention below, can give us a life of financial freedom, which can make us feel more secure about our future.

2 THE 10 DIGITAL PASSIVE INCOME THAT WE WILL MENTION IN THE BOOK

Among the following passive income, we have the following:

+ Social networks such as: Facebook, YouTube and Instagram (income through advertising)
+ Selling books through platforms such as Amazon KDP
+ Sale of Online Courses.
+ Portfolio income. Stocks
+ Streaming platforms: Twitch and Facebook Gaming
+ Creation of Apps: Admob and subscription income
+ Web pages

All these incomes can be monitored from your cell phone or from your computer.

That is to say, from your cell phone, you can see how your income flows to you.

There are other additional passive income such as ecommerce, affiliate marketing, among others, but I believe this 10 that we can already get an idea of what passive income we can choose to have.

3 SOCIAL NETWORKS

Social networks were born from 1995. As web pages, to reconnect with old friends, friends from school and university.

From 2002-2003, new social networks such as MySpace and LinkedIn appeared, which were more professional social networks.

Today we have various social networks, such as Twitter, LinkedIn, Facebook, YouTube and Instagram, but we will talk here about the 3 social networks that can generate passive income, which are Facebook, YouTube and Instagram.

In 2004, Mark Zuckerberg's Facebook appeared. Facebook currently has 2.5 billion active users per month.

In 2005 YouTube was born, where everyone begins to place YouTube links on their MySpace pages. It was later sold to Google. It currently has 2 billion active users per month.

Finally, Instagram, which was launched in 2010. It quickly

gained popularity among young people, allowing the sharing of photos and videos in real time. In 2012, it was acquired by Facebook.

It has approximately 1 billion active users per month.

Did someone say opportunity?

Well, these social networks can give us the opportunity to show ourselves to billions of people and show them our products or services.

These social networks can be the platforms that can catapult us to success.

If before the theaters and functions, it was where people were shown to the public, today social networks are.

They are the platforms that can catapult us to success, and make us known throughout the world.

And in addition, they can give us powerful passive income, below we will give details of each one.

Note: A new social network recently appeared that is causing an impact, its name is TikTok, but that I will not detail in this book.

3.1 YOUTUBE

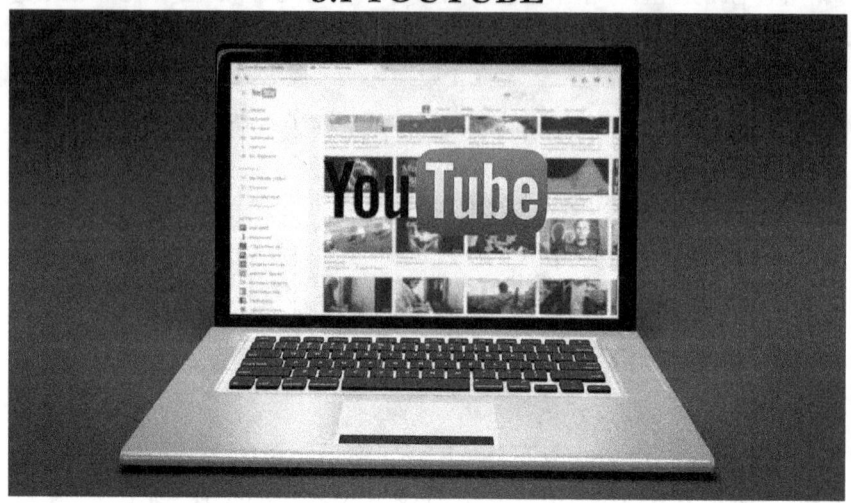

YouTube was created by 3 former PayPal employees in February 2005, in October 2006, it was acquired by Google, for 1.65 billion dollars. And the rest, as they say, is history.

It is a platform with 2 billion active users per month. (data from October 2020).

It was a social network that grew enormously, and the current result is that it generates millions of income in advertising, and also created a new type of millionaire, the famous "Youtubers".

These youtubers can be young teenagers between 15 and 25 years old, who talk about fun, games, challenges, or they can also be professional adults between 25 and 55 years old, who teach cooking recipes, coaching, mathematics, finance, etc.

Many of these youtubers became millionaires, they have millions of subscribers and millions of views.

YouTube is a platform that is in 76 languages, being in English and Spanish, the first and second predominant languages in this social network.

More than 70% of the reproductions come from mobile devices.

You can create a YouTube channel from the age of 13 or 14 depending on the country, with parental permission.

The videos that most attract the public are:

-people and blogs

-games

-entertainment

-music

-movies and animation

-educational

There are also channels on YouTube "how to do":

-how to make up

-how to cook

-how to exercise

and other things like that.

The recommendation is that you have a defined theme and based on it you create videos of this type.

Not everyone enters YouTube with the main idea of generating income through advertising, but of becoming known through the social network, to sell their brands, their products or companies.

That is, they use YouTube to make themselves known, be visible to their target audience, and later refer people to buy their products or services.

Today YouTube is a great opportunity to consider.

And if you have a business, you can, boost it on YouTube,

They can also give us considerable income.

Next, I will explain how you earn on YouTube.

PASSIVE INCOME ON YOUTUBE

YouTube allows you to monetize from:
- Of the 1000 subscribers
- And more than 4000 hours of playback

YouTube pays you under the modality of CPM. (Cost Per Thousand Impressions).

Let me show you the CPM of some countries.

COUNTRY CPM

Country	CPM
Japan	16$
Spain	11$
USA	11$
Australia	11$
Peru	1.76$
Colombia	2.65$
Brazil	1.24$

Source: My own research based on the resources and information provided by YouTube to its partners. (They are approximate data, I recommend that you do your own research, also that they vary with time, specific dates, seasons, etc.)

These are approximate data that I obtained, from my YouTube statistics in February 2021, remember that these vary and go up and down according to the seasons of each country. (like Christmas, special dates in each country, campaigns, etc)

We can see above all a trend, which is that English-speaking countries tend to pay more than Spanish-speaking countries, except for Spain, which is similar to English-speaking countries.

In other words, YouTube charges advertisers, say for example, $ 10 for every thousand views (this $ 10 amount varies by country, CPM is usually higher in English-speaking countries.)

YouTube pays you about 55% of that $ 10, which is about $ 5.

So how much would you earn if the CPM is for example $ 10.

If you speak English (USA, Australia)
1,000 views = $ 5 (half of $ 10)
1,000,000 views = $ 5,000

If you speak Spanish (Peru, Colombia)
1,000 views = $ 1 (half of $ 2)
1,000,000 views = $ 1,000

That is, with 1 million views you would earn $ 5,000 in the English-speaking market.

And with that same million you would earn $ 1,000 in the Spanish-speaking market.

There are other important factors as well that are taken into account to earn this amount of income.

And it is the relevance of the video, for the advertiser.

For example, if your channel is travel, and they have very good content, that is, quality content, advertisers will prefer to advertise with your channel, increasing your income.

If, on the other hand, the topic you touch is not so relevant for an advertiser, you could earn much less than what I mentioned above, despite having 1 million views

As I mentioned before, maybe while I was reviewing the statistics, some English-speaking countries had high CPM.

But on average according to my calculations, the English-speaking market tends to pay 3-4 times more than the Spanish-speaking market.

So if you speak English, you may notice that your language is a very important language in terms of income, in addition to being spoken on 5 continents.

In my case, my mother tongue is Spanish, which is why many of my videos are usually made in Spanish.

I also speak (and write) English, but it is not that fluent, and if you listen to me, obviously I would not sound like a native, so in some of my videos, I attach subtitles trying to reach to the English-speaking market, now you know why.

Who says that speaking languages is not important?

What are the advantages and disadvantages of YouTube?
ADVANTAGES
-Possibility of obtaining passive income through this platform.

-Possibility of becoming famous, through millions of reproductions and the virality that the platform can create for you.

- **The power of YouTube lies in the fact that people search for specific things on YouTube, when they enter YouTube they enter with an idea in mind**, for example they want to learn "digital marketing", they write it in the search engine, they want to "cook lasagna", too they write it in the search engine.

That is, YouTube is a social network used by people who directly have a real need and want to satisfy it by watching a video that can help them.

- The platform can generate passive income for you.

- By reaching so many people, you can literally become famous. That is why today we have famous youtubers that are known by millions of people, some of them are: Ninja,

Luisito Comunica.

These youtubers earn thousands and even millions of dollars in income from their YouTube videos.

DISADVANTAGES:

-Not everything is rosy, since, although there are youtubers that make millions, there are many others (perhaps 90%) that generate small income with this platform.

- One million views, it can generate you between $ 1000 to $ 5000 approximately. Although many YouTubers can achieve these figures without much effort, remember that 1 million views is a million views, and not all videos manage to generate this number of views.

If your content is in English, and you target an English-speaking audience, your income is usually higher, than for example the Spanish-speaking audience, which is usually smaller.

-The target audience you are targeting may not be so large, so you cannot get so many views (for example, if you sell or offer specific and specialized things), in this case I recommend that you use YouTube as a platform to Make yourself known more than to generate income.

SOME TIPS TO GO VIRAL ON YOUTUBE

YouTube allows you to reach thousands of people.

If you offer valuable content, you can become an authority in your area and become known YouTube, which is something very powerful for your business or brand.

Whether you want to obtain passive income with YouTube, or on the other hand you want to strengthen your brand using this platform, it is definitely an option that you cannot miss.

This platform also serves to redirect your potential

customers to your business.

Since on YouTube you can become a reference character in your area, and in this way attract customers for your business.

REQUIREMENTS TO MONETIZE ON YOUTUBE

We already mentioned it above, but we mention it again here.

-Comply with YouTube's monetization policies.

-Live in a country where the YouTube partner program is available.

-More than 1000 subscribers

- More than 4000 hours of playback

ELIGIBILITY FOR MONETIZATION

If you qualify, go to your channel, YouTube Studio, on the left side you search for monetization. And YouTube will tell you if you are eligible to monetize.

There are many people who achieve success on this platform, and the 1000 subscribers and 4000 hours are achieved in less than 1 or 2 months.

I have seen several youtubers grow like foam in less than a year, to 100,000 subscribers or a million.

But I have also seen how others who try to grow in this social network, remain stagnant and have problems growing.

I firmly believe that the most important thing to be successful on this platform is **that you have a defined theme,** be it "digital marketing", "kitchen", "mathematics", and **become a benchmark in that area.**

And the way to become a benchmark in an area is by giving high value content to your target audience, as well as quality videos, an additional fact is that your personality, your confidence, your security, the ability to transmit your message, also has powerful relevance when it comes to positioning your videos on YouTube.

Also tags or keywords are important when positioning your video on YouTube.

The people I follow are those who have more videos on a topic, for example let's say that the topic is digital marketing.

Who I follow is the one who has more videos on this topic, the quality of the videos he makes on this topic, and the person himself, his charisma, his way of speaking, his personality, etc.

EXAMPLE OF PASSIVE INCOME WITH YOUTUBE FROM THE CELL PHONE

We can see the passive income of YouTube from our cell phone.

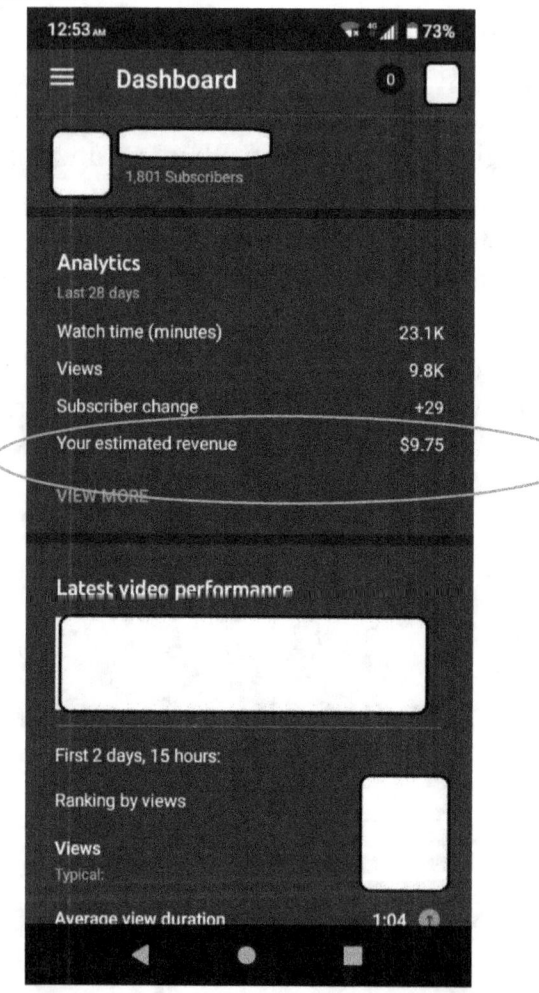

3.2 FACEBOOK

Facebook is another important player, which can also generate passive income for you.

The difference with YouTube is that when you search YouTube you are looking for something specific.

That is, you go to the magnifying glass, and write "how to cook", "marketing tricks", "what are business"

Instead, Facebook, "suggests" you.

You're walking through Facebook, and it says "hey max! You might like this video".

And it makes the suggestions, according to the things you follow, if you follow for example food videos, it will suggest these types of videos even more.

You could say that Facebook generates the need for you, while on YouTube you already have the need.

Take this into account when promoting your videos, your brand and your products.

Facebook pays slightly less than YouTube.

A strength of Facebook is that, if your video is of quality and generates engagement, the Facebook algorithm can make it viral.

A video goes viral on Facebook based on the number of likes, comments and shares they have.

If the Facebook algorithm sees that a video has these characteristics, what it does is "viralize" it and take it to people who have similar tastes.

The videos that are seen on Facebook are made through Facebook Watch.

The opportunity to generate income with Facebook is through instream ads (that is, while people are watching your video, an ad appears, for which the platform pays you).

You can post your videos on this platform, and if the video is striking, the platform will suggest it, if your video is getting likes, reproductions and shares, your video has the possibility of generating income and going viral.

ADVANTAGE

- is that the Facebook algorithm can make your video go viral, if Facebook denotes that video has engagement (that is, likes, shares and views.)

- Facebook is another important platform to generate income and make your business or product known.

-Remember that social networks not only serve to generate passive income, but to make your business known, or product that you promote.

- Facebook allows you to promote your fan page.

DISADVANTAGES

-Facebook usually pays a little less than YouTube, this is because not all Facebook video reproductions have ads, unlike YouTube where most video reproductions do contain ads.

REQUIREMENTS TO MONETIZE ON FACEBOOK

- More than 10,000 followers

- 30,000 1-minute views of videos of at least 3 minutes during the last 60 days.

- You need to create a fan page.

Otras herramientas de monetización
No cumples los requisitos para usar: Anuncios instream para videos a petición, Suscripciones de fans, Estrellas, Eventos online pagados y Administrador de colaboraciones de marca.

Anuncios instream para videos a petición
Los anuncios instream son anuncios breves que puedes incluir en tus videos para ganar dinero.
Cerrar requ ^

No cumple los requisitos

Aumentar el número de seguidores

1%

Seguidores
Esta página debe tener 10.000 seguidores como mínimo. Descubre nuevas maneras de ampliar tu público. Más información

Crear contenido atractivo

1%

Reproducciones de 1 minuto de videos de 3 minutos
Durante los últimos 60 días, necesitaste 30.000 reproducciones de 1 minuto de videos que duran 3 minutos como mínimo. Más información

ELIGIBILITY FOR MONETIZATION

If you manage to have 10,000 followers and 30,000 reproductions on your fan page, you go to Creator Studio, click on monetization, select the instream ads tab (which are the ads that will appear within your videos) which will generate income.

EXAMPLE OF PASSIVE FACEBOOK FROM PC

We can see in this example, what is paid to this channel for its revenue from advertising (or instream ads), that is, within your videos Facebook places ads for which it pays you.

3.3 INSTAGRAM

As I write this, the Instagram platform is testing new features including Reels. used to make short videos of less than a minute.

Likewise, YouTube is testing the shorts platform, which is the same as short videos

As I write, Instagram still does not monetize its ads, that is, Instagrammers do not earn money from the videos they make, this may change because it had been announced that IGTV was going to pay Instagrammer.

So how does an Instagrammer generate income?

The main way they have managed to earn income is through publications / posts, brand promotions.

If, for example, you have 10,000 followers, you can charge approximately $ 100 for a post, promoting a business or company or a businessman.

If you reach 30,000 followers, you can earn income of $ 300 and up.

There are Instagrammers or also called influencers, who can earn thousands of dollars, because they have millions of followers on this platform.

This is the way that many Instagrammers have managed to obtain thousands of dollars, many of them also create their own brands and their own stores.

So it is an option to take into account Instagram, the platform is currently being updated, due to the recent competition from social networks, makes these platforms update.

The recent novelty of Instagram are the Reels, which are short videos of less than 60 seconds, which can be seen by thousands of people.

ADVANTAGE

-The advantages are that Instagram has a large young audience that can increase traffic to your website or product, it also allows you to reach new audiences.

-Another advantage is that Instagram makes use of hashtags or tags, if you have these tags in your photos or videos, you can attract the public organically, and get hundreds of views. Likewise, with the Reels platform you can upload short videos, have thousands of people see you on Instagram.

DISADVANTAGES

Among the disadvantages we have that the platform, at the moment they still do not pay they do not pay income to their Instagrammers, as I mentioned they generate their income through post or publications.

Well, those are the three most important sources of passive income when it comes to social media.

Recently the social network TikTok appeared, which is a recent phenomenon.

Social media can give you a passive income.

You don't need to have a lot of programming knowledge.

What is needed is to have a topic to talk about, a camera, know a bit of editing, handle tags, keywords, orient yourself to a niche.

Many youtubers are not successful on YouTube because they tend to play many songs at the same time.

The recommendation is to touch on a subject in depth and become a reference in that subject.

If you are a reference, people will want to listen to you.

This is what I have seen with many channels, which have grown like foam.

For example, channels that teach Japanese, channels that teach Chinese, some channels that talk about travel, only touch on these specific topics.

If you play several topics at the same time, for example, business, then you talk about music, and then you talk about travel, people are going to get confused.

4 KDP AMAZON – BOOKS

Auto Publish with Amazon KDP

KDP AMAZON is a self-publishing platform that allows you to put a book for sale in Amazon stores around the world in its 3 formats:

- Ebook version (Kindle and Kindle Unlimited)
- Softcover version (printed)
- Audiobook version (With Audible platform)

For every sale you make on this platform, Amazon pays you royalties.

For you to write a book you simply have to go to Amazon, KDP, open an account, and start publishing books.

In the printed version, **Amazon works in the form of**

print-on-demand, that is, if a user buys your book, the printing of your book just begins, from the moment of user payment.

Amazon sends it out to print, and then ships it in two or three days to the person who bought your book.

If it is a digital version, it is easier, since once they buy your book, the buyer has access to your book in its digital format.

For the audiobook version, **we have Audible, which is a platform that for a subscription allows users to listen to audiobooks.**

By registering your book in audible, you can also earn considerable income and in some cases even higher than the Ebook and paperback formats.

The online book sales system is currently highly automated.

In other words, basically all you have to do is write the book, layout it, create a cover for it, and Amazon takes care of the distribution and delivery.

In the case of the audiobook, they can create it with the ACX platform that is from Amazon.

You can also promote the sale of your books, through ads in the Amazon store, so that people can buy your book.

So basically what you need to do is:

-write the book

-make it up

- Create a cover (You can have it done for $ 10 or $ 15, on platforms like workana or fiver, and have a professional cover)

-And add advertising that is optional, but is necessary if you want to boost the sales of your book.

-Amazon is in charge of the distribution and printing.

You can write your book in Word.

Or you can also do it on platforms like professionals like Adobe InDesign.

To publish an Ebook, you are asked for the text document (Word, or pdf) and a simple cover.

In the case of a soft cover book, you will be asked for the text document, and a cover and a back cover.

In the case of the printed book, Amazon will follow the specifications you gave it and will print the book and send it later to the person who bought your book, as I mentioned this part is completely automated.

You can also convert your book into an audiobook, it can be listened to by thousands of people. This through Amazon's Audible platform, which has grown enormously in recent years.

So, with self publishing books, we have three ways to generate passive income, there are many people who make thousands of dollars selling books.

If you manage to position your book, among the best sellers, you can earn considerable passive income.

TIPS TO SELL BOOKS IN AMAZON

An important tip when selling books on Amazon. It is selling books that are in high demand.

Many people enter the world of self-publishing writing books that they would like, but without seeing the demand, and the end result is that their book does not sell, and they have spent maybe weeks writing their book, this could demotivate them and believe that it is not sold on this platform.

For this reason, the tip of selling on demand, you can see in the Amazon store, which are the best-selling books and write books that have that theme.

If, for example, you see that the topic, business is in high demand, you can write related to that area.

Or you can also write in sub-niches and become a reference on that topic.

This is basically a market study.

To see if there is demand for what you want to sell before writing your book.

Companies do the same, when making business plans, first they do a market study to see if their product will be in demand and based on this they decide whether or not to produce and distribute their product.

Same for the books on Amazon. The advantage is that the market study in Amazon is simpler, since Amazon makes a list of its best-selling books, which you can take as a reference to choose the subject of the book or books that you can write.

ADVANTAGE

-We have a fully automated platform once you create the book (and mock it up and put a cover on it) you don't have to do anything else, Amazon takes care of the rest.

-Amazon is the largest platform for the sale of books in the world. Which is a great opportunity to have a market of millions of people to whom you can sell your book.

-It allows you to have passive income once you made the effort to write the book, layout it, publish it, and advertise it. Once you have finished the whole process you can earn passive income without doing practically anything else.

-Amazon is the number 1 platform for selling books.

-Writing a book increases trust in your clients, and your

credibility as a professional, if you know what you are talking about and writing about, and it can also position you as a "reference" in your area.

A clear example of obtaining real income with this platform is my real experience: a few months ago, in the afternoon I slept for a while, and when I woke up I saw that I had made several sales, automatically. While sleeping! can you believe it?

Do you think that in other eras that I mentioned earlier (the industrial age and the agrarian age) this was possible?

Well no.

So it's a great opportunity

If you like to read and you like to write this may be a great opportunity for you.

It is also an opportunity to enhance your professional growth, since writing a book gives you proof that you are an expert and a reference in your area.

For example, if we compare a real estate specialist, which one would you prefer?

The one who has five written books talking about the different areas or functions of his activity, or the one who has no written book.

Well, most of us would prefer the one who has more books, because he would possibly have sales of his book, and would make us think that if he sells it is because he knows what he says.

And even more so if his books are best-seller.

In the future it is possible that the business cards will be discarded and the new business cards will be the books of each one, it is your best image in front of clients.

A card can be thrown away, a book hardly.

It can generate you great income.

On average according to my calculations:

-30% of the book value is earned.

For example, if your book is worth $ 9, on average you would be earning $ 3, if we take away from those $ 9 what are taxes, and the printing, you would be earning in the end about $ 3. (It could be a little less if invest in advertising)

If your book happened to be a boom and you sell 1000 copies of your book a day, and you sell it for $ 9.99, you would be earning roughly $ 3,000 a month according to my calculations. (It may vary depending on the results you get when paying for advertising)

As we can see, it is a great opportunity to generate income, once the book is created, all the work is done, what remains is to promote it and Amazon is in charge of distribution and printing.

This is one of the ways that I earn passive income.

And believe me it is very satisfactory, when you enter your sales reports, and you see that you have sold books!

If you want to increase your income, you would have to write more books, but once the whole process is done, you could already enjoy passive income.

DISADVANTAGES

-Not everyone likes to write.

-In some niches, there is a lot of competition, and it can be difficult to sell books and make a profit from the sale of your books.

-When you write your book geared towards very small niches, it may generate little or no sales.

-In some cases when investing in advertising, you may not cover your costs, generating losses.

However, after all, KDP is a good option to generate passive income and there are many people who generate thousands of dollars with this platform.

ADDITIONAL DATA

There are many people who have made substantial income writing books ranging from $ 2,000 to $ 10,000 per month.

In no passive income, which I mention, success is guaranteed.

They all carry a risk, a learning curve, but all of them also have the possibility of generating passive income.

Amazon is the largest market, so imagine that you sell about 500 books a month, you would be generating roughly $ 1,500 a month in passive income.

There is the case of authors who self-published their books, and they became famous and known worldwide, and in some cases their books reached the cinema, although there are few cases of this type, they have also occurred.

If you want more information about this fascinating world of self-publishing **you can join my group on Facebook: Passive Digital Income or follow me on my social networks.**

EXAMPLE OF AMAZON KDP PASSIVE INCOME FROM PC

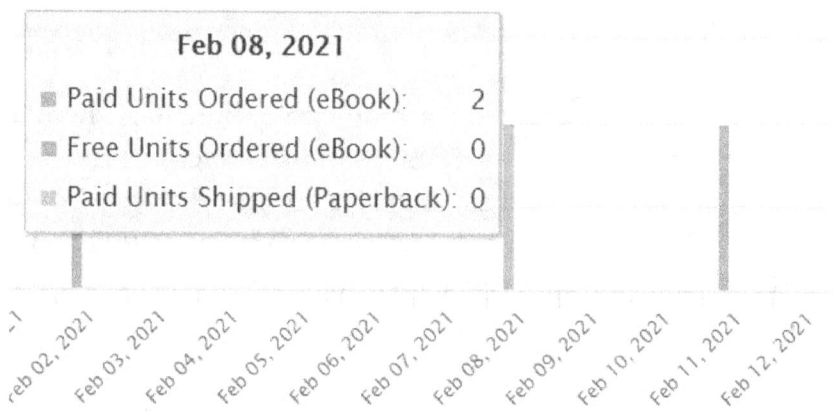

Royalties Earned (What's this?) ∨

Marketplace	Currency	eBook Royalty	Paperback Royalty	Total Royalty
Amazon.com	USD	6.91	7.72	14.63
Amazon.co.uk	GBP	0.00	2.44	2.44
Amazon.de	EUR	8.85	5.16	14.01
Amazon.fr	EUR	0.00	0.00	0.00
Amazon.es	EUR	0.33	0.00	0.33
Amazon.it	EUR	0.00	0.00	0.00
Amazon.nl	EUR	0.00	0.00	0.00
Amazon.co.jp	JPY	888.00	0.00	888.00

5 SALE OF ONLINE COURSES: PLATFORMS LIKE HOTMART, UDEMY AND OWN PLATFORMS.

Well, we move on to the infoproducts / online courses.

You can sell courses, mentoring and workshops online.

If you are, for example, a psychology professional, you can sell a course for couples, or for families to overcome problems.

These course and workshop platforms can be fully automated, meaning that once the system is created, all you have to do is monitor it.

This is a bit more difficult to master, because to earn passive income in this way, you need to master the following areas:

-Facebook Ads or YouTube Ads

-digital marketing

-remarketing

-email marketing

-Management of Cookies

-Creation of webpages

-Hosting Management

-Purchase of domains, among others.

As you can see, you basically need knowledge in digital marketing and web design.

The courses can be sold through different platforms.

We have at least three types of platforms:

- The first can be Udemy, which is a platform that sells courses, the same platform sometimes promotes your course to other people, but it usually charges high sales commissions.

-We have the Hotmart platform where you can upload your courses, the platform charges you a commission for each sale made.

-You can buy a space to give to upload your videos of your course in exchange for a monthly payment, like the Teachable platform, in this case they no longer charge you commission, but you would have to make a monthly payment to keep your course on the platform. This would be a good option if you have a considerable number of students.

If you can master this passive income, you can have a reliable and constant source of income, and as I explained once created, it can be completely automated. What would be done basically, after having created your course, is to monitor it, to see that your spending on advertising is less than the sales you make of your course.

And see how profitable for you is the sale of courses or workshops.

Advertising is important when selling courses or workshops online.

For example, imagine that you create a guitar course. You created it, good. And what happens after?

Well, nobody, buy your course, because nobody knows it exists!

That is why I mention that it is important to invest or advertise, or attract your clients through social networks that mention lines above such as Facebook, YouTube and Instagram.

Advertising is done through Facebook Ads. In other words, you pay Facebook to show your ad on its platform.

If you used Facebook, I am sure you have seen dozens of advertisements selling you different types of products.

In this case, it is also necessary to have a web page, to be able to filter potential clients, and give them "gifts" and valuable content so that they finally buy your course.

ADVANTAGE

- The pros of the infoproducts course is that you achieve success, you can earn great income, there are people who manage to earn thousands of dollars, between $ 2,000 to $ 10,000 or more.

-These platforms can be fully automated, and once created, your main function is to monitor your advertising campaign.

-You can automate this type of business 100% or almost 100%.

-If you are a professional in an area, for example "real estate", you can take advantage of your expertise, and teach and transmit it to other people eager to learn.

- You can become a benchmark in your field by creating

courses for thousands of people.

DISADVANTAGES

-There is a barrier to entry due to the knowledge it demands, such as digital marketing, web design, among others.

-In most cases you need a website, which can cost you between $ 30 to $ 50 a month.

-There are also very competitive sectors in this industry.

-You can generate losses, if the cost of your advertising is lower than your sales of your product.

Additional data

This type of passive digital income is also one of my favorites, and another that I master, if you want to know more about this type of passive income, I invite you to follow me on social networks or join my group on Facebook "Passive Digital Income".

What I like about this type of passive income, despite the fact that it takes time at the beginning, and is demanding in terms of knowledge of digital marketing and web pages, is that once created, you only dedicate yourself to monitoring it. It is like a machine that generates money automatically.

I teach different courses, in different areas that I master, I have a Digital Marketing course aimed at creating workshops, another course to Sell successfully on Amazon, among others

EXAMPLE OF PASSIVE ENTRY OF ONLINE COURSES OF THE HOTMART PLATFORM FROM THE CELL PHONE

HOTMART POCKET

Venta efectuada
Tu comisión: US$ 29

HOTMART POCKET   Hace

Venta efectuada
Tu comisión: US$ 4

HOTMART POCKET   Hace 25 min

Venta efectuada
Tu comisión: US$ 1

HOTMART POCKET   Hace

Venta efectuada
Tu comisión: US$ 1

In the case of the Hotmart platform, these types of notifications usually reach your cell phone every time you make a sale.

Did someone say they want passive income?

6 PORTFOLIO INCOME, STOCK AND DIVIDENDS

Stocks and dividends.

Dividends have been around since the industrial age.

Since companies to reward their investors, they began to pay dividends.

The reason I mention them is because today, the purchase and sale of shares can be done with a single click, and the payment of dividends is done automatically, and it is deposited into your account.

Many years ago you had to physically go to buy or sell your shares and also to collect your dividends.

Today all this is done with a single click.

There are several authorized platforms, such as Interactivebrokers, and Ameritrade.
That allow you to easily collect and sell shares.

2 types of income:
Stocks can give you 2 types of income:
-Capital gains (when the share goes up in price), or capital losses (when the share goes down in price).
-Dividends, you are paid a percentage of your share each year, which is usually between 1 to 8%.

That is, if you have $ 100, you can earn between $ 1 to $ 8 per year in dividends.
It doesn't sound very sexy right.
However capital gains in some cases are usually very high.
This is the case, for example, of Tesla shares, which, at the beginning of 2020, were worth $ 100, and at the end of December 2020, they were worth $ 800, a gain of 800%.
Imagine if you had at that time had $ 10,000 in tesla shares, at the end of the year, you would have made $ 80,000.
Obviously, this book is not to give investment advice, I am not saying that you buy Tesla shares, each one should do their respective research.
Since you can also lose money.
The focus of this book is to see the opportunity to generate income.
The stock market is a place where there is an appetite for risk, and where money can be made or lost.
Many people enter it, because they love to invest, and they seek financial freedom.
Dividends and stocks can give you financial freedom if you can build a portfolio that pays you dividends, which would

be the passive income that helps you cover your long-term expenses.

In order to live on your passive income from stocks, you need to build a long-term portfolio, and reinvest your capital gains and dividends.

For example, if over the years, of hard work and investment, you will manage to have a portfolio of approximately $ 200,000, and that entire portfolio pays you 4% in dividends, you would be receiving passive income, worth:

200,000 * 4% = $ 8,000 annually.

Warning: You have to be very careful with this type of investment, and it is not recommended for everyone.

Since it involves risk and it is necessary for the person, in this case the investor, to be well informed so that they can make good decisions and not lose money.

Since as we know, as the market rises, it also falls, and when it falls, many people can lose a lot of money.

So in this case, I recommend a lot of study, research, in this matter, in order to make good decisions.

As I repeat this book, it is not to give investment advice, but to show the opportunity for passive income.

In none of the passive income that I show, success is guaranteed, however, it is a great opportunity.

ADVANTAGE

- Passive income can be obtained through dividends
- Today the platforms that sell shares are highly automated, and you can buy and sell shares with a single click and the payment of dividends is made automatically and is deposited into your account.

DISADVANTAGES

- It is a source of long-term passive income, where you have to build a portfolio to obtain passive income through dividends.
- Just as you earn a lot of money, you can also lose a lot of money, so I recommend a lot of study and research.
- It takes a certain amount of capital to buy shares. There are actions that cost $ 20, but others can cost up to $ 2,000.
- You need to have a source of income, so that you can buy stocks, since you need to build a long-term portfolio. (That is, your income can come from your work or your business and with them acquire shares to build your portfolio.).

If you like the stock market, and you are aware of the movements that large entrepreneurs and companies make, this type of passive income could be for you.

The stock market is a place where people looking for freedom, but it is also a place where there is also a lot of risk, if you do not know what you are doing.

EXAMPLE OF PAYMENT OF DIVIDENDS FROM PC

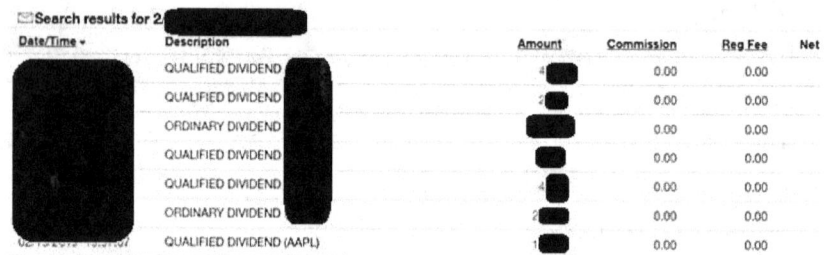

Dividend payment

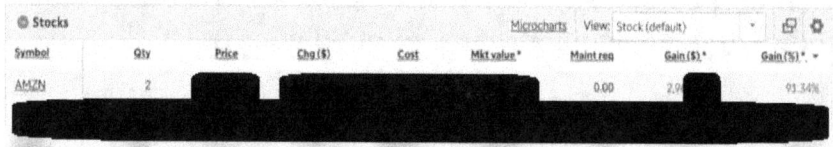

Capital gains on stock

7 STREAMING PLATFORMS, TWITCH AND FACEBOOK GAMING

Streaming platforms have become very important in recent years.

These platforms are very popular, especially in 2 areas:

-**Video games**: Streamers play various video games or a single game that many people like.

-**Just Chatting**: The streamers are dedicated to transmitting different things, talking to users, cooking, dancing among others.

We currently have 2 major platforms dedicated to streaming, they are Twitch and Facebook Gaming.

Streamers earn their income from donations and subscriptions

This type of income is not totally passive, it is a semi-passive income.

Since it needs your presence to be able to receive donations and subscriptions.

There are many streamers, who have a large following, and who can earn a lot of money.

So let's start with each platform:

7.1 TWITCH

Twitch was created in 2011. And it is owned by Amazon.

It started out as justin.tv, allowing people to stream live video online

Justin TV finally in 2011 created a platform for the gamer community because this niche was growing enormously, Twitch was finally created in 2011.

Today Twitch is the most important platform in terms of online streaming.

In 2014, Justin TV was shut down and the company focused entirely on Twitch. According to data from the platform in 2020, Twitch received approximately 17 million visitors per day, and an average audience of more than 1.5 million viewers.

Streamers generate thousands of dollars with this platform through two mechanisms:

- the first is donations, that is, people donate money to their favorite streamers.

-the second is subscriptions, people subscribe to their favorite streamer's channel for $ 4.99, in exchange for emoticons, and also to support their favorite streamer.

This income is semi-passive, in the sense that sometimes people subscribe to your channel for 8 months (which have not yet elapsed), that is, they have generated income for which you will still have to transmit in the coming months.

Many streamers broadcast live on Twitch, then post their videos to YouTube.

The advantage of online streaming is that people can ask questions and interact with their favorite streamers in real time.

Many youtubers switched to Twitch to broadcast live due to the potential of the platform.

It is a great option to consider due to the number of users who use the platform and the considerable number of subscribers and donors that exist on the platform, who donate to their favorite streamers.

Some streamers can generate thousands of dollars, with this platform.

If games are your thing, or you want to do live broadcasts to be seen by thousands of people, this platform could be for you.

ADVANTAGE

- Among the advantages as I mentioned is a large market of people who are willing to donate and subscribe to their favorite streamer.

-It can generate you considerable income, broadcasting on the platform.

DISADVANTAGES

- You need a computer or a computer with good features to stream, since it consumes a lot of data. You need a good video card, a good GPU, and good RAM. These specifications are necessary to be able to do a good quality live broadcast.

- A good internet connection is necessary for good quality transmissions.

- It is a very competitive platform and to have quality followers and subscribers you need to give your audience a quality channel

It is a competitive platform, but if you succeed you can earn thousands of dollars with this platform.

7.2 FACEBOOK GAMING

Facebook gaming was launched in April 2020.
Facebook allows broadcasts through Facebook Gaming.
With Facebook gamers can do live broadcasts, hold events and play video games.

ADVANTAGE

- The Facebook algorithm makes suggestions, and if it sees that a channel is well received, it can recommend it to the millions of Facebook users.

- For a set amount of money, you can buy stars and donate them to your favorite streamers, which makes some streamers earn considerable income.

DISADVANTAGES

- It is similar to Twitch, it requires a good internet connection and that your computer has good specifications for proper transmission.

- There is competition on the platform and many users seek to position themselves with their channels.

As I mentioned, both platforms give you semi-passive income, since to donate it is necessary that you are streaming.

8. CREATION OF APPS

This type of passive income is the most complex of all those mentioned in the book.

We have 2 platforms where these apps are created:

-The IOS platform, owned by Apple.

-The Android platform, powered by Google.

Android was released in 2008. It was designed for mobile devices such as cell phones, tablets, and televisions.

Android has the Google Play platform where there are 1,500 million active Android devices and 2,000 million monthly users on Google Play.

In 2018, they racked up 115 billion in-store downloads in the last twelve months.

Passive income is obtained in 2 ways:

-Through ads (which pays you per CPM that I mentioned on YouTube)

-Through subscriptions to your app, your app can offer some unique or necessary service, for which users would pay to have the features that the app offers them.

In order to create apps, you need to know programming, which is difficult for most people outside of this industry.

Another alternative could outsource the manufacture of the app to a company, from countries like India, which usually charge you between $ 2,000 to $ 5,000 per application.

Let us remember that this is the way in which new millionaires are born, through the creation of applications for computers or cell phones.

Thus were born the billionaires of Facebook, WhatsApp, Instagram, and YouTube.

If you dream big, this could be the way to earn big passive income for yourself.

If you were to create or own an app, with millions of users, you could be the next millionaire or billionaire.

I particularly have a name for the applications, I call them, "21st century real estate."

Every time you have a user in your app, each user is like an "avatar" within your world (of your app), each person is like a little piece of monopoly within your app or world,

if you have millions of people who use your, then your app could literally be worth billions of dollars.

ADVANTAGE

-This type of passive income can make you reach millions of people

-It can earn you substantial passive income if you reach millions of people

DISADVANTAGES

- It has strong barriers to entry, including mastering programming, or having the capital to outsource an app to an app creator.

- Even when you develop your app, it may not be in demand, or it may be in a very competitive niche.

I have developed a couple of apps. One of them is called "learn Quechua", and the other is called "easy kana" to learn hiragana and katakana from Japanese.

Both are available on the playstore. Both apps have less than 1000 downloads.

It took me several months to learn the basics of programming, and it's not easy, and I also consider myself a novice in this area.

However, I wanted to try. And so, I managed to develop both applications with great effort.

9 WEBPAGES

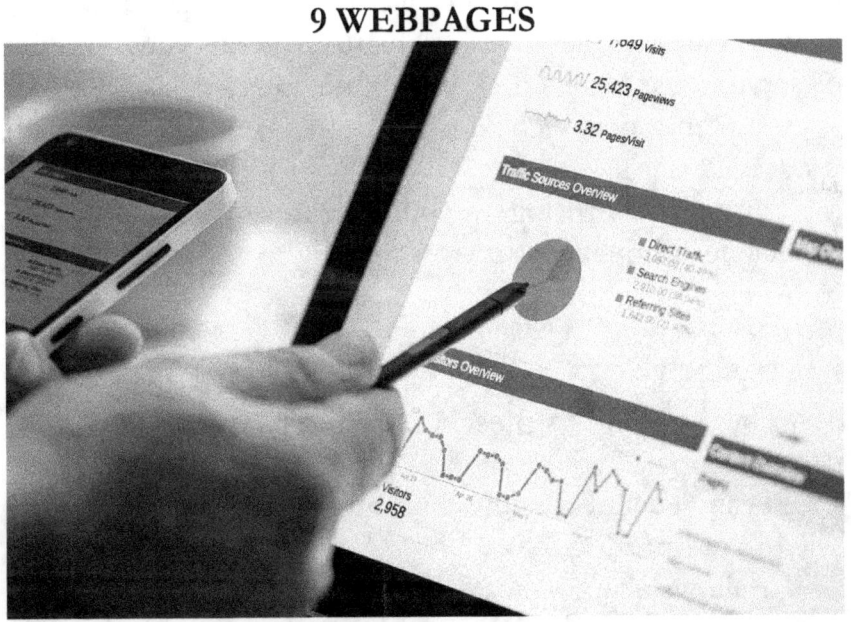

Before social networks, web pages were very popular. They allowed you to obtain passive income through advertising on your website (with Adsense).

Web pages had a great boom in the 90's. With the birth of social networks, they lost a bit of relevance.

Nowadays, a web page can be made in a simple way, with platforms such as WordPress and wix.

However, these revenues have been slowing down a bit, due to the competition that web pages have with social networks such as YouTube, Facebook, among others.

A website today is important, if you have a business or a company. Since most people, before doing business with any company, they tend to first "google" it, to find out what type of company it is, what service it offers, and how big it is.

Web pages are also important to promote your product or service, and have a presence on the internet.

As I mentioned, web pages can earn you income through 2 ways:

-Through advertising on your website (Adsense).

-Selling products or services directly from the company's website.

ADVANTAGE

- They give you a presence on the internet, since most people "google" you

- It can generate income through advertising or the direct sale of your product

- It allows you to create funnels, that is, you can direct potential customers to your website, and with it, give promotions and discounts to this potential audience to buy your products or services.

DISADVANTAGES

- It has a monthly cost between $ 30 to $ 50, because you need a hosting and a domain for your website to operate.

- You can create a website for free with platforms like blogspot, but this gives a poor image to your company.

SUMMARY

These are the various types of passive income that we can have with the Internet, from our home or office and that can give us financial freedom, I know people who earn thousands of dollars and who are references in each of the passive income that I have mentioned.

There are book experts on Amazon, who can make anywhere from $ 10,000 to $ 30,000 per month.

There are people who sell courses in digital marketing, coaching, productivity and who also earn thousands of dollars, if you are a professional, you can take advantage of the info-products and sell your product to a wide group of people, the decision is in your hands,

Well, we also have the Dividends as we explained, there are many people who have managed to obtain a considerable portfolio and live comfortably with the dividends that they generate.

We can see that there are many options to generate income that can be obtained from the comfort of our home or office, just by having the internet and a computer.

There are several mentioned in this book, because I don't know them very well, some of them are affiliate marketing and ecommerce, but I think that with the ones I mentioned you can already get an idea of the opportunities we have with the internet.

Today we are in new times, in the middle of the coronavirus pandemic, generating income from our house is an option that can be very important to us.

Robert Kiyosaki author of Rich Dad Poor Dad, in his

book mentions that in this new information age there will be people who will cling to old ideas and will be relegated, while another group will generate thousands or millions of dollars taking advantage of new opportunities for the age of information.

I made this book with the intention of showing you the different types of income that you can generate if you have a computer and an internet connection, I hope it has been useful to you.

The most surprising of all these income mentioned, is that you can monitor them from your cell phone or computer, while you are, for example, traveling, eating, and even sleeping.

You could literally be on a beach, and people could be buying your book, your course, or watching your YouTube videos, you could see the deposits of your dividends in your bank account, and see how passive income flows to your bank account .

So welcome to the information age, to the new normal, and to the opportunities that this information age offers us.

You can join my Facebook group called "Passive Digital Income" or follow me on social networks, to share more information about the passive income that I master and that I like the most.

Remember that it is easier to achieve a goal when you work as a team.

In this book I was not able to go into great depth with each of these topics. But it wasn't the end of this book either.

My goal with this book is that you can see all the alternatives that we have at our disposal and that you can choose, given your skills and preferences, the one that suits you and you think can give you the passive income you want.

If you are interested in knowing more, you can consult me on my social networks.

so that I can explain the three that I master the most, which are Amazon KDP, online courses, and managing social networks, through digital marketing.

I hope this book has been helpful to you, I want to thank you for getting here and I hope you make the decision to choose the vehicle that will lead you to earn the passive income you want.

As I usually say "you are at a passive digital income to achieve the income and financial freedom you want.

The END.

FINAL NOTES

You don't need to be successful in all of these areas, just one to get the income you want.

remember there are many famous youtubers making thousands of dollars.

Some people can only use one of the vehicles mentioned. Others may use a mixture of all of them.

I hope this book has been of great help.

Join my group on Facebook "Passive Digital Income"

There I will share information about the different types of passive income.

We are waiting for you, we upload information and resources related to passive income.

My favorite passive income is the generation of income through books, courses and management of social networks through digital marketing.

If you want to join my group or have information about the 3 courses I teach:

-Amazon KDP course,

-Course to promote your product or service,

-Digital marketing course aimed at generating passive income.

You can also follow me on social networks.

Many people do not even know that these opportunities that the information age brings us exist, or they believe they are scams, lies, or impossible to achieve.

But out there, making thousands of dollars, on every single digital passive income I mentioned.

Again, you are one passive digital income away from achieving the financial freedom you desire.

ABOUT THE AUTHOR

Max Chahua is a Peruvian coach, and a CPA.
He has written books about languages, economics,
productivity, finance, Coaching and Accounting.
After working in the banking industry, and in the Real
Estate industry, and finally in the Accounting industry.
He began his consultant career, where he mentors
entrepreneurs in tax and fiscal matters.
He also loves technology, has taken courses and seminars
on digital marketing, has created applications available in
the play store, like "easy kana" to teach Hiragana and
Katakana Japanese, and "aprende quechua", to to teach the
traditional peruvian language.
He offers courses where he teaches digital marketing, self-
publishing in amazon, and courses where he teaches how
to sell your products or services in automatic.